ABCs at Home

T0100907

Daniel Nunn

Raintree

Chicago, Illinois

www.capstonepub.com
Visit our website to find out more information about Heinemann-Raintree books.

To order:

☎ Phone 800-747-4992

💻 Visit www.capstonepub.com to browse our catalog and order online.

Edited by Dan Nunn and Rebecca Rissman
Designed by Joanna Hinton-Malivoire
Picture research by Ruth Blair
Originated by Capstone Global Library Ltd
Production by Alison Parsons

Library of Congress Cataloging-in-Publication Data
Nunn, Daniel.
ABCs at home / Daniel Nunn.
p. cm.—(Everyday alphabet)
ISBN 978-1-4109-4731-4 (hb)—ISBN 978-1-4109-4736-9 (pb) 1. English language–Alphabet–Juvenile literature. 2. Home–Juvenile literature. I. Title.
PE1155.N86 2012
428.13—dc23   2011043705

Acknowledgments
We would like to thank the following for permission to reproduce photographs: Shutterstock pp. 4 (© glo), 5 (© Arvind Balaraman), 6 (© Alex Staroseltsev), 7 (© pick), 8 (© Peter zijlstra), 9 (© Africa Studio), 10 (© Losevsky Pavel), 11 (© 101imges), 12 (© Neveshkin Nikolay), 13 (© Jessmine), 14 (© Elena Elisseeva), 15 (© cosma), 16 (© Val Thoermer), 17 (© sonya etchison), 18 (© Poulsons Photography), 19 (© Anson0618), 20 (© VectorZilla), 21 (© Karkas), 22 (© g215), 23 (© hfng), 24 (© krsmanovic), 25 (© Elnur), 26 (© swinner), 27 (© Alina Bakker), 28 (© lorenzo_graph), 29 (© Ruta Saulyte-Laurinaviciene), 30 (© mmPhoto, © Illman), 31 (© MaxFX, © norinori303, © natu).

Cover photograph of a child's bedroom reproduced with permission of Shutterstock (© Pablo Scapinachis).

Every effort has been made to contact copyright holders of any material reproduced in this book. Any omissions will be rectified in subsequent printings if notice is given to the publisher.

Contents

The Alphabet. 4

Find Your Own ABCs at Home 30

Index 32

Aa

armchair

An armchair gets its name because it has sides you can rest your arms on!

B b

bath

Baths are fun AND important! You need to have a bath often so you can stay clean.

Cc

clock

Clocks tell us what time it is. This clock says it is ten minutes past ten.

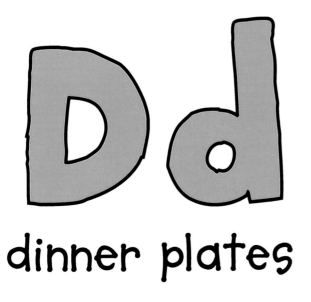

Dd

dinner plates

We eat our meals off dinner plates. Without dinner plates, meal times would be very messy!

7

Ee

egg cup

An egg cup is a special cup made just to hold a boiled egg.

8

flowers

You can make any home feel brighter with pretty flowers in a vase.

9

Gg

garage

Some homes have a garage. You can keep a car in a garage.

Hh

hangers

Hangers keep your clothes neat and tidy in your closet.

11

Ii

iron

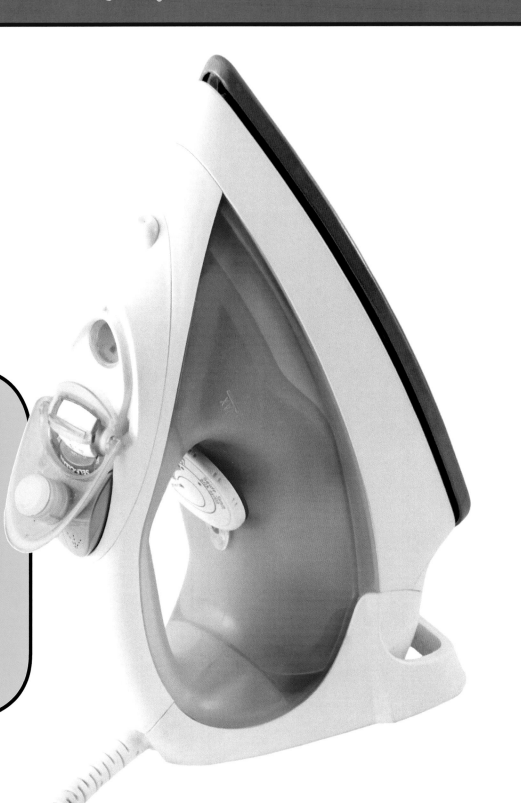

You use an iron to get rid of creases in clothes. Never touch an iron. It might be very hot.

Jj

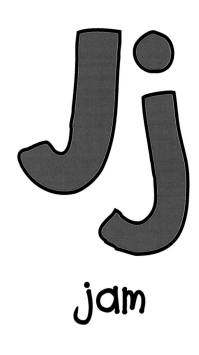

jam

Jam comes in jars. Both "jam" and "jar" begin with a "j."

13

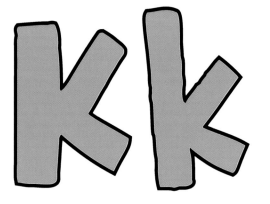

kitchen

We make our meals in a kitchen. This kitchen looks very clean and tidy!

Ll

light

A light helps us to see things when it is dark.

15

Mm

mirror

You can see what you look like in a mirror. It shows you your reflection.

16

Nn

neighbors

Your neighbors are the people who live nearby.

Oo

oven

We bake food in an oven. Ovens are very hot! Never use an oven on your own.

plant pot

A plant pot holds flowers and other plants. Remember to water your plants regularly!

Qq

quilt

A quilt will keep you warm and snug in bed at night!

Rr

rug

A rug is a small carpet. It makes a hard floor more comfortable—especially for cats!

21

Ss

sink

We wash our hands in a sink. Always wash your hands after you have been to the bathroom.

Tt

television

You can watch lots of different programs on a television. What is your favorite TV program?

upstairs

Some homes have an upstairs and some homes do not. Does yours?

Vv

vacuum cleaner

A vacuum cleaner sucks up dust and dirt to keep floors and carpets clean.

Ww

window

Windows let in light so we can see in the daytime.

26

xylophone

A xylophone is a musical instrument you play by hitting it with a stick.

27

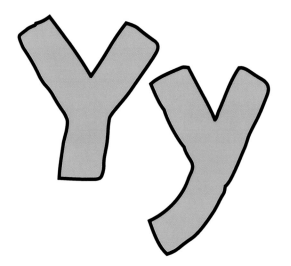

yogurt

Yogurt is a food made from milk. It comes in different flavors! Do you like yogurt?

Zz

zipper

Zippers are used to close things. Lots of clothes have zippers. Can you think of anything else that has a zipper?

29

Find Your Own ABCs at Home

Can you find your own ABCs at home? How many different things beginning with each letter can you find? Here are some ideas to help you!

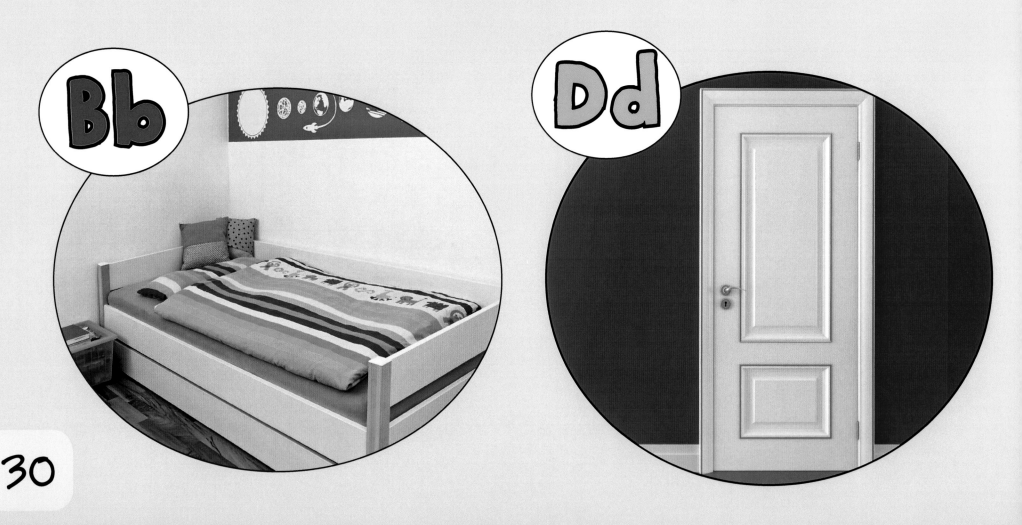

Bb

Dd

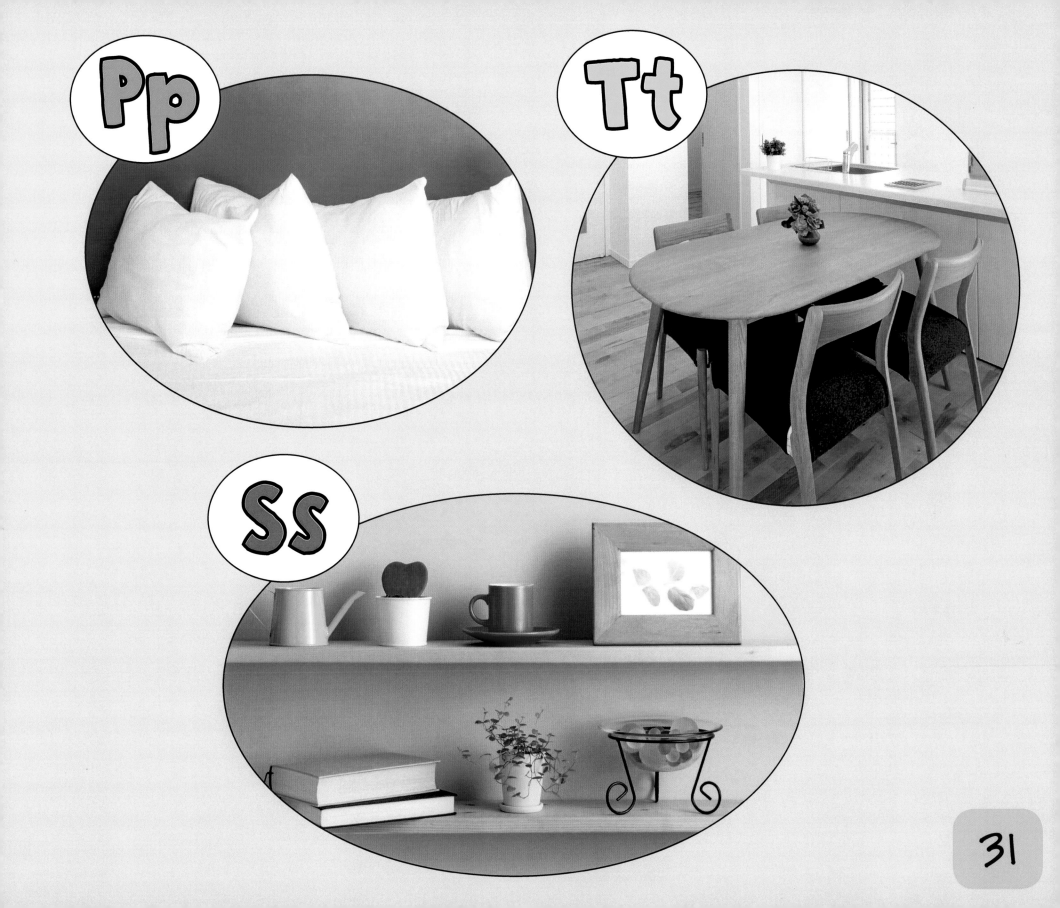

31

Index

armchair 4

bath 5

clock 6

dinner plates 7

egg cup 8

flowers 9

garage 10

hangers 11

iron 12

jam 13

kitchen 14

light 15

mirror 16

neighbors 17

oven 18

plant pot 19

quilt 20

rug 21

sink 22

television 23

upstairs 24

vacuum cleaner 25

window 26

xylophone 27

yogurt 28

zipper 29